Fifty Easy
Classical
Guitar Solos

Arranged and edited by **Jerry Willard**.

Cover photography by Randall Wallace
Project editor: Peter Pickow

Order No. AM 949058
US International Standard Book Number: 0.8256.1729.4
UK International Standard Book Number: 0.7119.7612.0

Exclusive Distributors:
Hal Leonard
7777 West Bluemound Road, Milwaukee, WI 53213
Email: info@halleonard.com

Hal Leonard Europe Limited
42 Wigmore Street, Marylebone, London WIU 2 RY
Email: info@halleonardeurope.com

Hal Leonard Australia Pty. Ltd.
4 Lentara Court, Cheltenham, Victoria 9132, Australia
Email: info@halleonard.com.au

Printed in EU.

www.halleonard.com

Fifty Easy
Classical
Guitar Solos

Contents

Selected Composer Biographies

Fernando Carulli was born in Naples, Italy on February 10, 1770, the son of a famous statesman. Carulli's first musical instruction was on 'cello; however, he was soon attracted to the guitar. Carulli was entirely self taught as a guitarist, yet he rapidly became known as one of the leading virtuosi of his day. In 1808, he moved to Paris where he was to make his home for the rest of his life. He was an extremely prolific composer, writing a great number of solos as well as chamber works for the guitar. Carulli died in Paris on February 17, 1841.

v

Matteo Carcassi gained great renown in the nineteenth century due to the publication of his method and numerous studies for guitar, which remain highly regarded and quite popular to this day. He was born in Florence, Italy, in 1792 and acquired an extraordinary guitar technique at a precociously early age. In 1820 he moved to Paris, which became his home. Carcassi concertized throughout Europe and became known as one of the great guitar virtuosi of his time. He died in Paris in 1853.

v

Fernando Sor is considered to be the most important nineteenth-century composer of works for the guitar. He was born in Barcelona, Spain, February 2, 1778, the son of a well-to-do Catalan merchant. Sor received his first musical instruction at the monastery of Montserrat. At eighteen, he composed his first opera, *Telemachus on Calypso's Isle*, which was produced in Barcelona in 1797 to tremendous acclaim. In 1812, Sor moved to Paris and established himself as a great guitar virtuoso and composer. It was around this time that the music critic Fétis dubbed him "the Beethoven of the guitar." He made his London début in 1815 to great acclaim, and, in 1820, he moved to Russia where he produced three ballets. In 1830, Sor published his famous *Method pour la Guitar*, one of the finest methods ever written. He died in Paris on July 8, 1839.

v

Dionisio Aguado was born on April 8, 1784 in Madrid, Spain, and died there on December 20, 1849. He studied music at a college in Madrid where a monk named Basilio taught him guitar and the elements of music. Later on he worked with the renowned singer/guitarist Manuel Garcia from whom he obtained a thorough knowledge of the resources of the guitar. In 1803, Aguado moved to Aranjuez, where he devoted homself to the further study of the guitar. It was during this period that he developed a system of fingering and harmonic effects that became his *Method*, which was published in Madrid in 1824. Aguado moved to Paris in 1825, where he became friends with the great guitar virtuoso Fernando Sor. In fact, Sor wrote the beautiful "Les deux amis" in celebration of their friendship. In 1838, Aguado returned to Madrid where he spent the remainder of his life.

v

Francisco Tárrega is known as Father of the Modern Guitar, and was among the most important figures in guitar history. Tárrega was born on November 21, 1850 in Castellon, Spain. His first guitar studies were with local guitarists, and at the age of eleven he played a concerto by Julian Arcas in his native town. In 1874, he entered the Madrid Conservatory where he was awarded first prize for harmony and composition. Upon his graduation he traveled to many important cities on the Continent, receiving critical and public acclaim for his guitar virtuosity. He was a great teacher, and many of his students—such as Miguel Llobet and Emilio Pujol—became famous in their own right. Many of Tárrega's excellent compositions remain a vital part of the modern guitarist's repertoire. He died in Barcelona, Spain, on December 5, 1909.

v

John Dowland was born in 1562 and is generally considered the greatest lutenist/composer of the late Renaissance. Dowland traveled a great deal, and he lived in Denmark, Germany, and Italy as well as his native England. He is known for his beautiful lute songs and solo lute compositions. Dowland was appointed to the court of James I in 1612, a post he held until his death in 1626.

v

Wolfgang Amadeus Mozart was born in Salsburg, Austria, in 1756. Mozart was the greatest musical prodigy the world has ever known. He wrote his first piece when he was five, and at twelve years of age was writing full-scale operas. He was a prolific composer and is one of the most important figures in music history. The "Petit Piece" included in this collection is an early work which lends itself quite well to the guitar. Mozart died in Vienna, Austria, in 1791 at the early age of thirty-five years.

v

Lesson

Fernando Sor
(1778-1839)

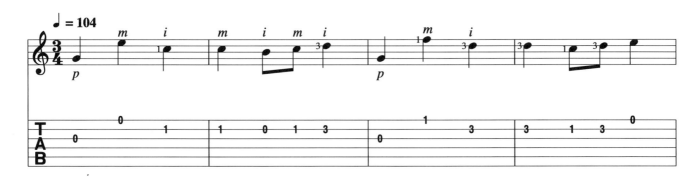

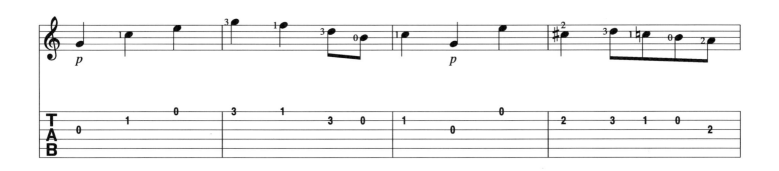

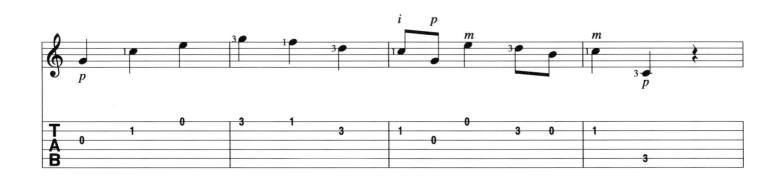

Study in C

Fernando Sor
(1778-1839)

♩ = 100

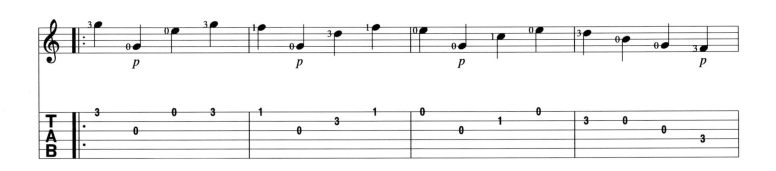

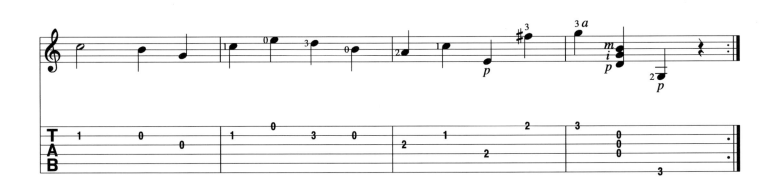

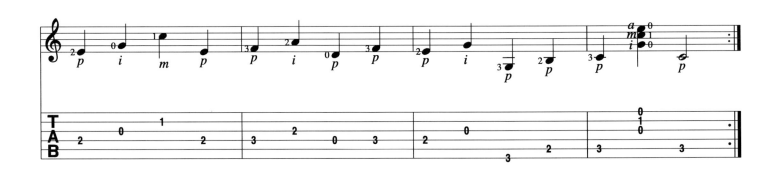

Andantino

Joseph Küffner
(1776-1856)

Andantino

Joseph Küffner
(1776-1856)

Waltz

Dionisio Aguado
(1784-1849)

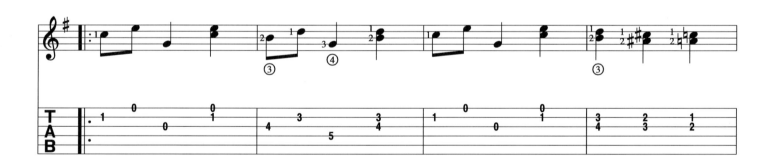

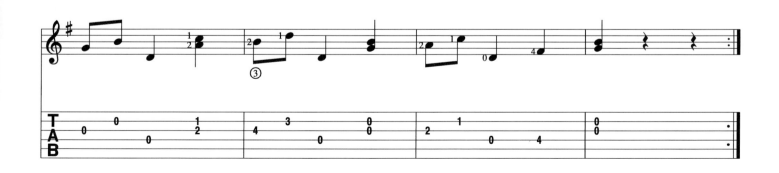

Andantino

Matteo Carcassi
(1792-1853)

Waltz

Ferdinando Carulli
(1770-1841)

Study

Ferdinando Carulli
(1770-1841)

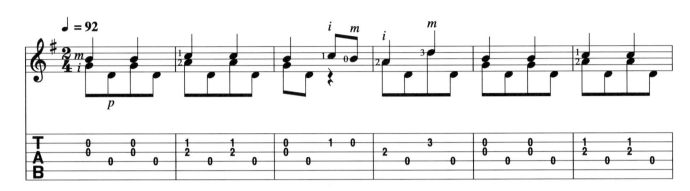

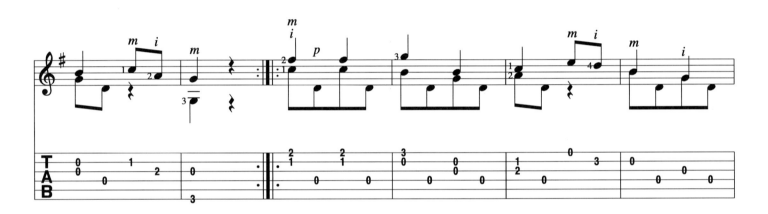

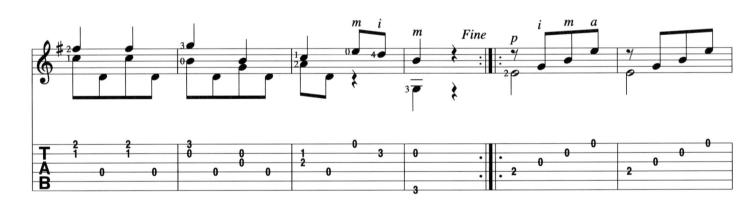

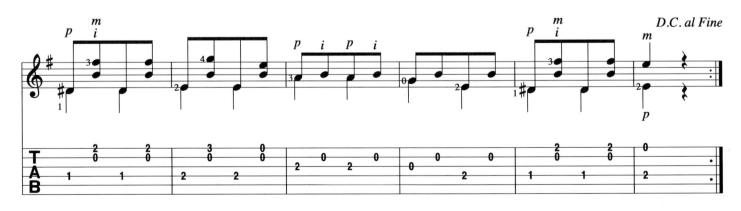

Andantino

Fernando Sor
(1778-1839)

Andante

Fernando Sor
(1778-1839)

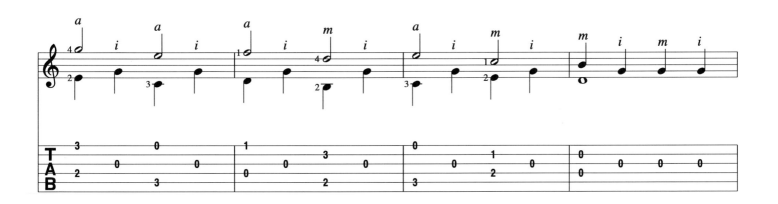

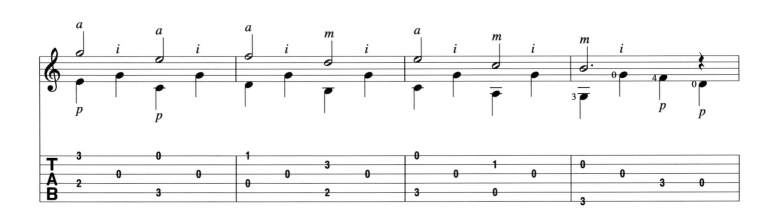

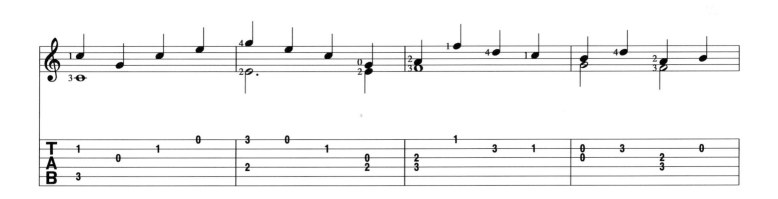

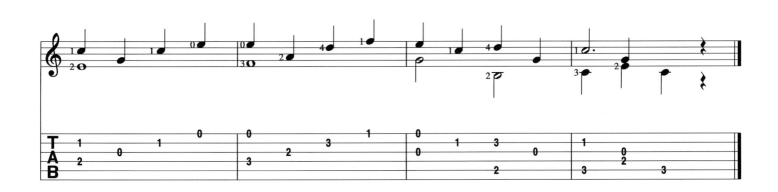

Andantino

Mauro Giuliani
(1781-1829)

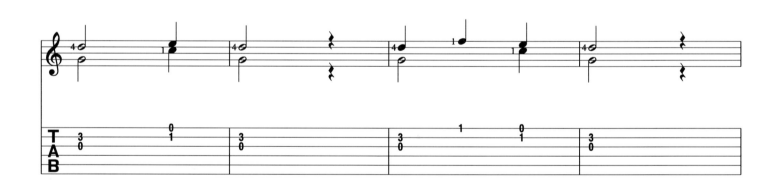

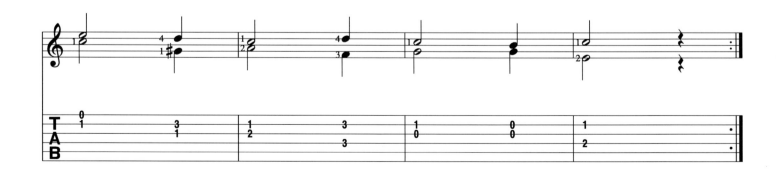

Nonesuch

Anonymous
17th century French

Waltz

Ferdinando Carulli
(1770-1841)

Allegro

Mauro Giuliani
(1781-1829)

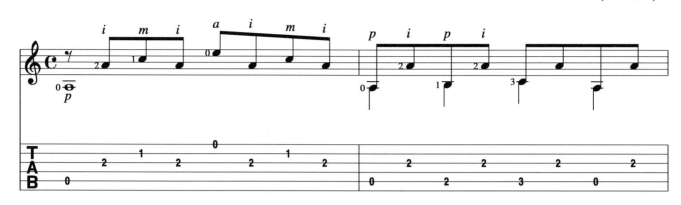

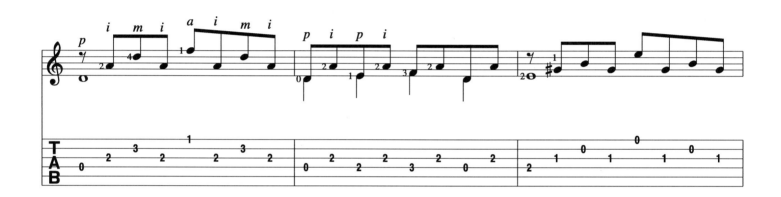

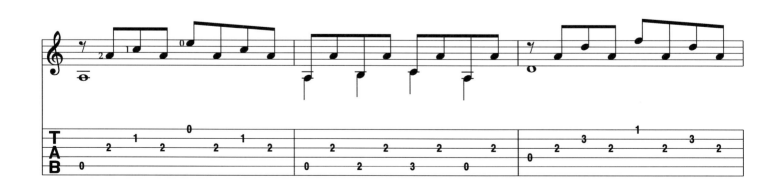

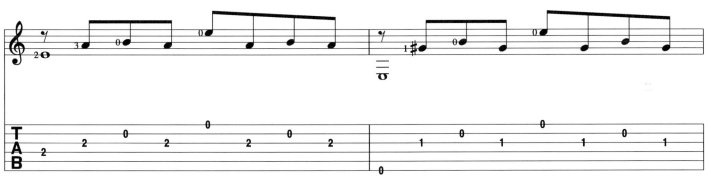

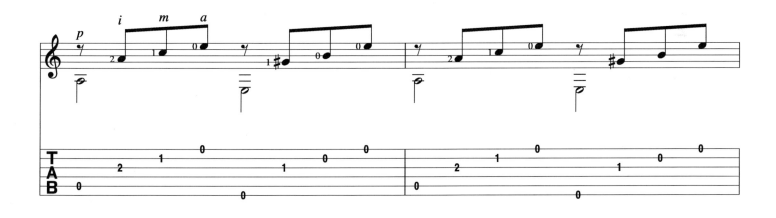

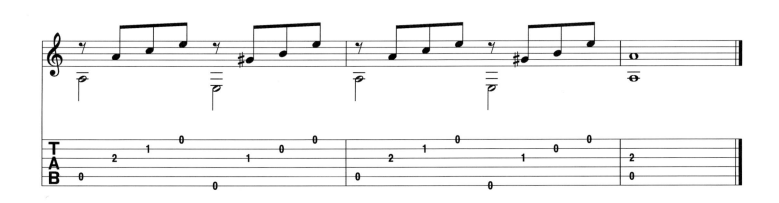

Andante

Fernando Sor
(1778-1839)

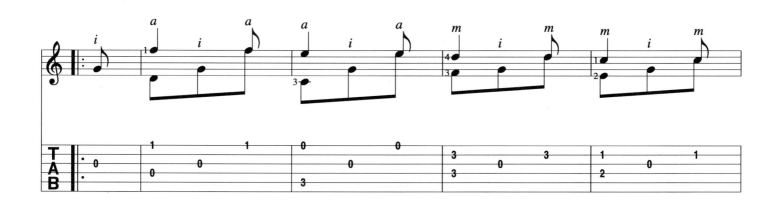

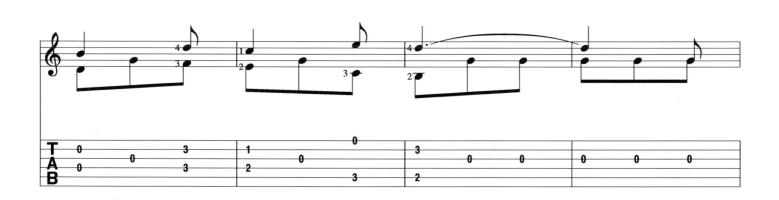

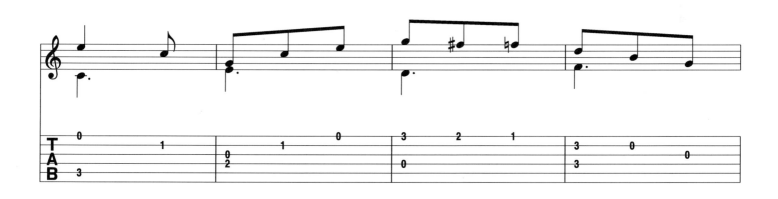

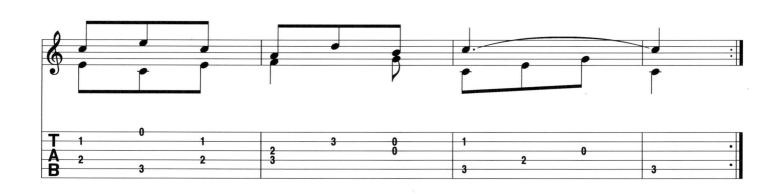

Branle

Anonymous
16th century

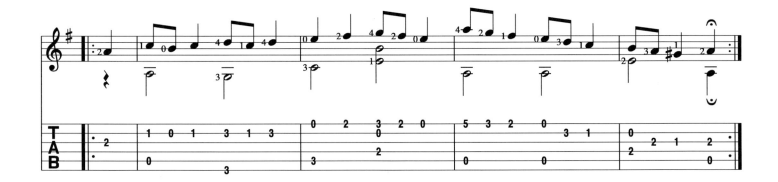

Allegro

Ferdinando Carulli
(1770-1841)

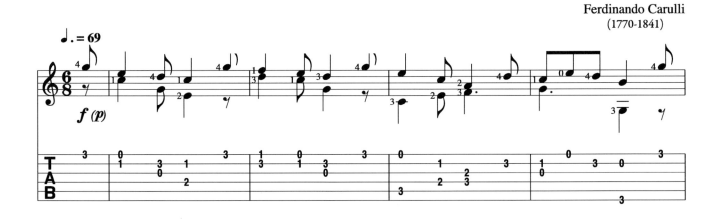

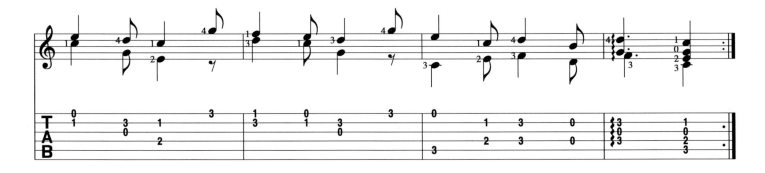

Andante

Matteo Carcassi
(1792-1853)

Study

Fernando Sor
(1778-1839)

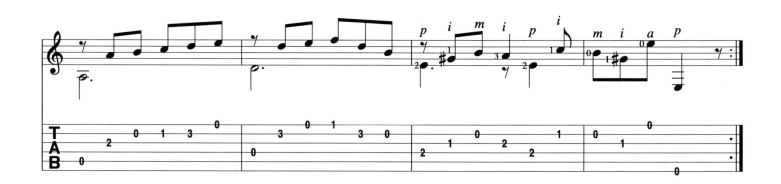

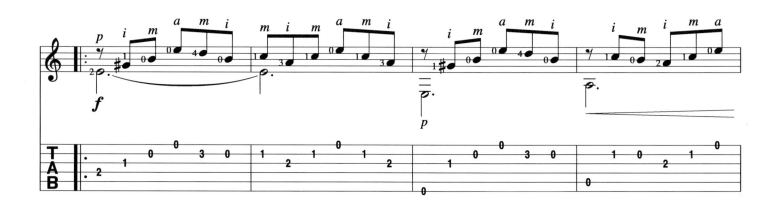

Minuet

Johann Krieger
(1651-1753)

Lesson

Fernando Sor
(1778-1839)

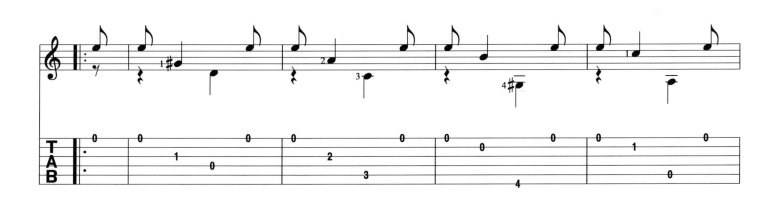

D.C. al Fine

Andante

Fernando Sor
(1778-1839)

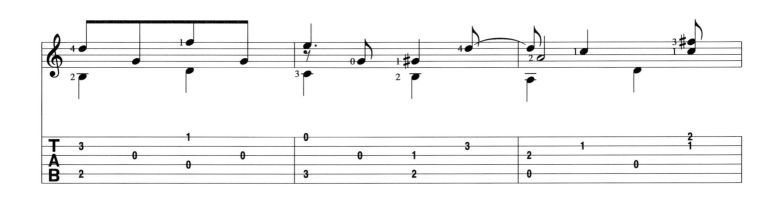

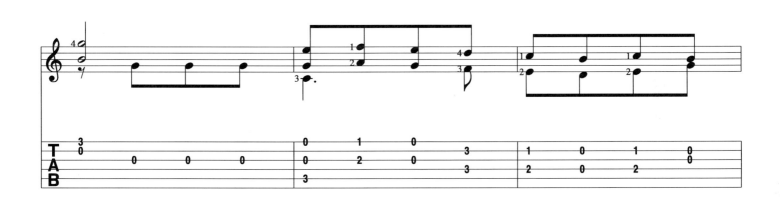

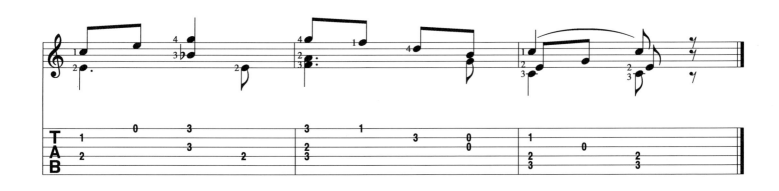

Moderato

Fernando Sor
(1778-1839)

Allegretto

Fernando Sor
(1778-1839)

Andante

Ferdinando Carulli
(1770-1841)

Allegro

Mauro Giuliani
(1781-1829)

42

Españoleto

Gaspar Sanz
(1640-1710)

Study

Dionisio Agaudo
(1784-1849)

What If a Day a Month or a Year

Anonymous
16th century English

Rujero

Gaspar Sanz
(1640-1710)

Contradanza

Fernando Ferandière
(18th century)

Copyright © 1999 Music Sales Corporation (ASCAP)
International Copyright Secured. All Rights Reserved.

Minuet

Robert de Visée
(1660-1720)

Volte

Anonymous
16th century English

Allegretto

Mauro Giuliani
(1781-1829)

Greensleeves

Anonymous (attributed to Henry VIII)
(1491-1547)

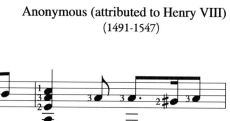

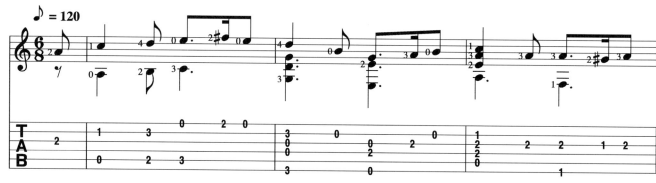

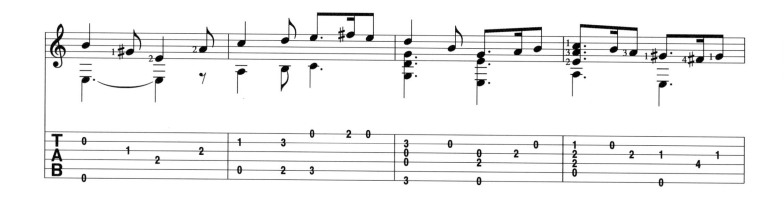

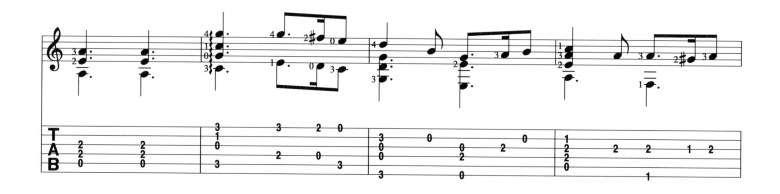

Bourée

Johann Krieger
(1651-1753)

Study

Mauro Giuliani
(1781-1829)

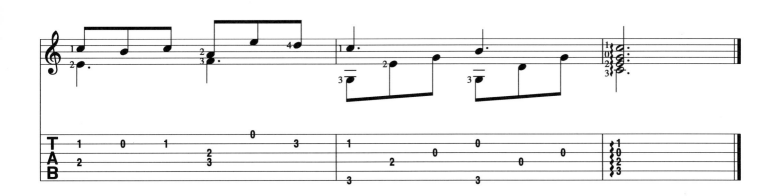

Mrs. Winter's Jump

John Dowland
(1563-1626)

Bourée

Leopold Mozart
(1719-1787)

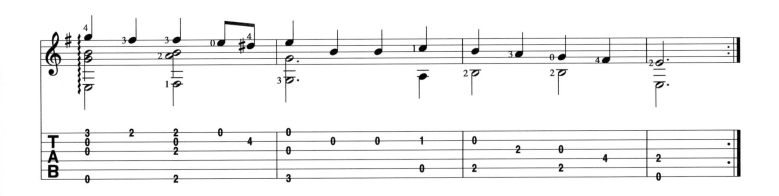

Andante

Fernando Sor
(1778-1839)

Moderato

Fernando Sor
(1778-1839)

Andante

Fernando Sor
(1778-1839)

D.S. al Fine

Allegretto

Fernando Sor
(1778-1839)

Packington's Pound

Anonymous
16th century English

Petite Piece

Wolfgang Amadeus Mozart
(1756-1791)

Andantino

Fernando Sor
(1778-1839)

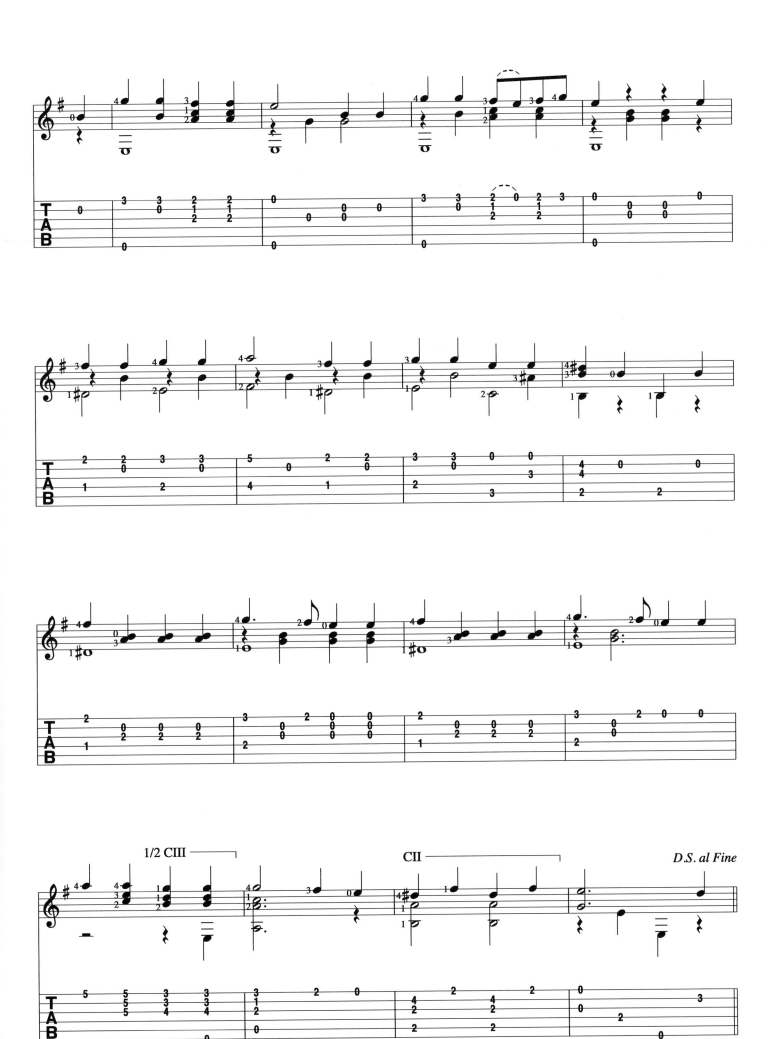

Andantino

Fernando Sor
(1778-1839)

Andante

Fernando Sor
(1778-1839)

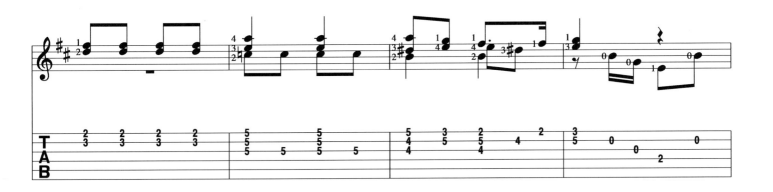

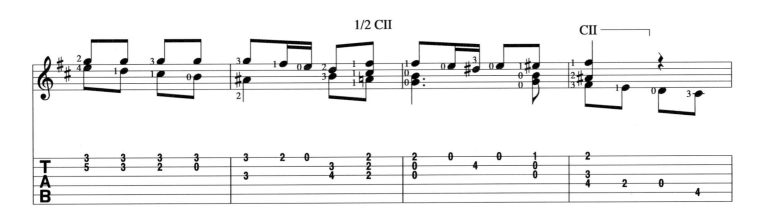

Estudio

Francisco Tarrega
(1852-1909)

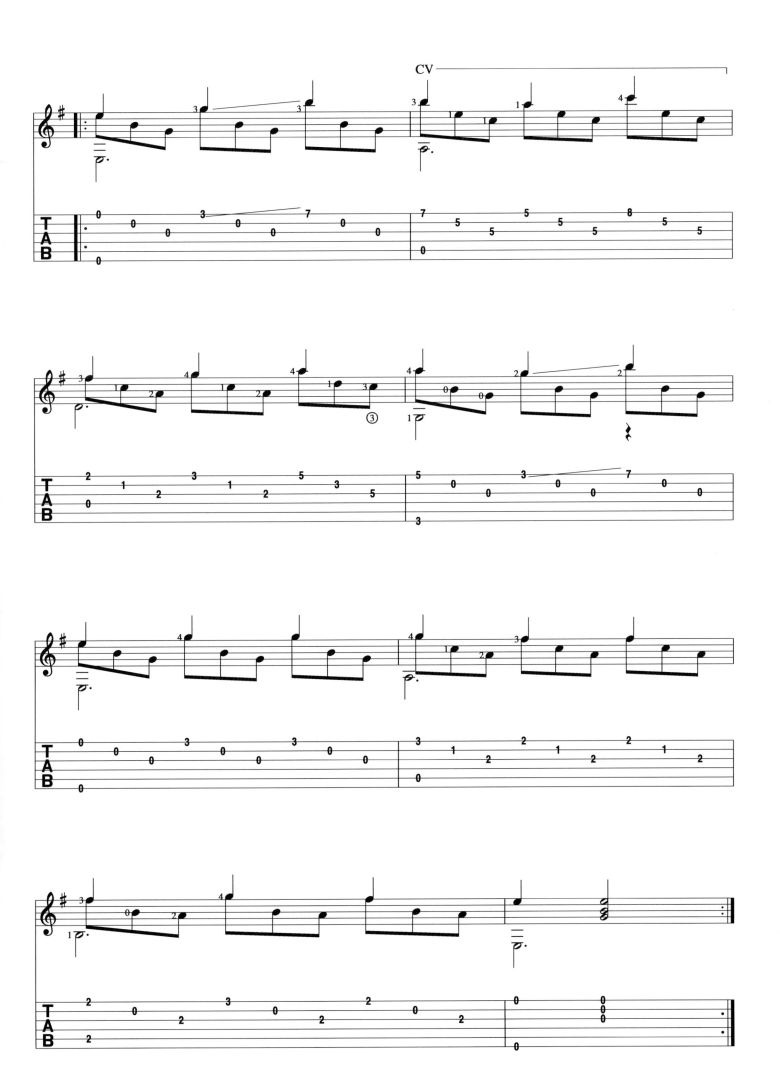

Minuet

Robert de Visée
(1660-1720)